The Dead River Poems.

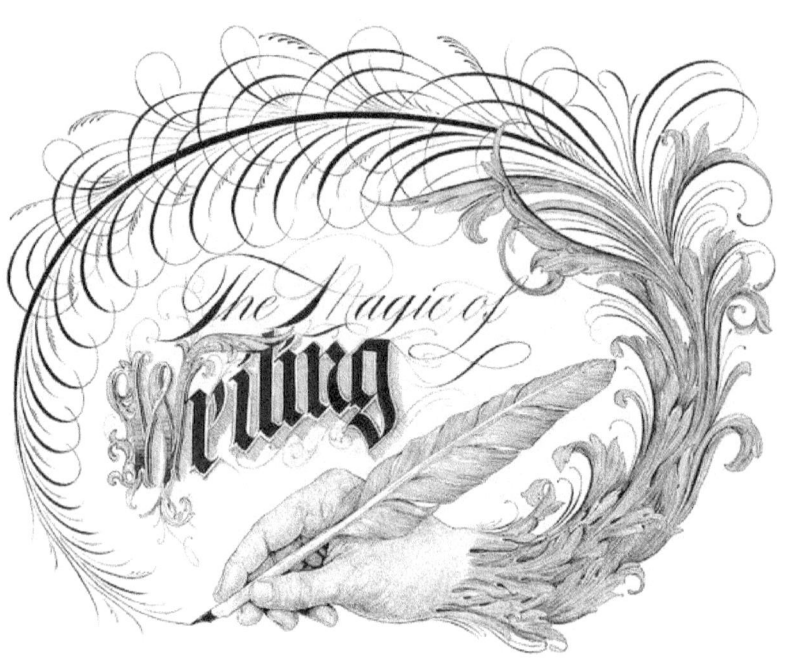

Writers are no better than any one else
and yet they reach for the unattainable without regret.
With a vision that sets them far apart, they allow line after
line to spill across far to many discarded pages.
Here they form tales that rhyme with wit, merit, sorrow
and laughter, all while taking time to look past reflections of
their own beliefs that echo back for others to believe that they
too can survive.

That my friend is the magic behind Creative Writing.

This compilation of poems has been inspired
by a two year struggle in writing the book-
Dead River Falls.

Some are from the story line itself,
while others were merely inspired by the memories therein.

G.W.Crider

The Rapid River.

Far be it for men to dream of things
or for women to knit their sweaters seam.
If it not be that the latter mattered,
then it should be forgotten as well.

For whom can recall a rushing stream
where rocks get tossed;
skimming under its cold surface
'till they becomes lost
beneath an ever darkening depth
of a light above?

Each skip and bob resounds
with a thunder of promises

which try to rob dignity from the day.
While every rippling quake brings joy-
along with it, a smile
in this quiet place.
Within this bright radiance
the forest comes alive
for all to taste...

Here we can grow!
For here- we know,
we're not alone.
It shines with absolution
and hope for love.
Just like those
who traverse a rapid river.

Heading for the Unknown.

Let the world outside do as it will,

for I will do the same.

I'll head into the unknown head first

while never second guessing a thing.

After all,

it has taught me this much;

anxiety is a bitch.

I've seen the good and bad,

the known and things skeptical enough

to even consider believing and yet,

I've survived.

Footprints in the Heart.

Blinded by ambitions.
Enveloped with adoration's.
Wrecked by sights of inhibition;
a beautiful hurt that leaves a mark.

Pressures building from indecision,
all while making decision after decision;
and this is as good a place as any
to start making footprints in the heart.

Table of Mystery.

Beneath a forest thick with thieves

lies within a cavern a key.

Through darkness in solitude it sits quietly;

allowing its blackness to unfold

a great mystery.

No stars to rise upon a moist shrine.

No reprieve, only endless time.

Hereby bones rest below in disguise.

And to this end alone,

the real quest will spill wonder upon

unsuspecting eyes.

Nature calls to exclude the exhumed.

As those worthy fight to find this hall.

To learn once again how to stand tall.

To soon it rises;

moon after moon looms to a backdrop of falls.

Here it waits - silently ready,

for any who transgress this room.

Enlightening it is in a matter of things.

Encroaching maybe;

but we were once kings.

Encouraging yet, frightening;

it was set to liven skilled beings.

So welcome to this table -

this table of mystery.

Diving in Deep.

Pools of the heart are deep, shallow,

and at times, wholeheartedly mistaken...

As if the tides of the moon

knew who we were,

we should come alive

and dance in its radiance.

We should therefore dive in,

wading 'till we find its deepest parts.

There we can learn to except sinking,

or we can hold unto beauty,

thus giving into its whim.

Lady luck.

An honor it's been
to seek my immortal twain-
furthermore in recognizing
what's remained.
It's been a game of chance,
a flip of a coin;
even more so,
it's kept me sane.

Bartering life for love
to become divine
takes more than a single lifetime.
And then to carry this weight
between halves is a burden
that soon comes to pass.

All while what's clogged remains
and stays unsure of its worth;
there will always be these tidings,
some claim it a curse.

And yet, there is a difference,
something that's much,
much worse.

It is to live without searching,
or even seeking to see;
that one cannot become whole
without showing reverence
unto the lady.

Where the Cold Wind Blows.

Through reality's gaps
we call on fate to navigate
things we cannot comprehend.
And yet, we choose,
in part, what is believed
as it leads to sequestration
in the end.

Let us chase our dreams
together at night if need be.
Following the rapid waters
that flow deeply into parts unknown.
Awakened and eager to leave
the world we knew behind.

Core Difference.

Though tender love may be,
the softer side is in the eyes.
Now don't get me wrong!
I'd roll in the hay all day
to get a glimpse inside,
then sit back and sigh —
I get lost in the eyes.
Oh, those wonderful eyes.
They speak what the heart cannot.
Whispering sweet lullabies
to the core of difference.

Divided.

Since when have we become so divided?

Some would say the left caused this,

others would claim the right but,

I'm here to say,

we were divided long before this!

We became divided as a whole

when we rejected each others opinion over our own.

As if we knew it all,

and no one could tell us otherwise.

Let's face it, we've become soap box hero's

trying to be heard over the crowd.

Maybe there's still time to listen.

Maybe there's even time to learn before we finally rest.

And maybe if we exercise a touch of restraint

as we listen to our neighbor,

and then respond in kind,

we may survive as a race...

Maybe.

A Fresh Start.

I may be a bit compulsive in my thinking.
It may even seem repulsive but,
I can't get past the word Had.
It's a past tense feeling that makes me sad.
Was I not good enough to hold on to?
Was I only a passing fad?
Either way I look at the word,
I lose a bit of myself.
My confidence fades.
Maybe it's just my wayward thinking but,
I'll be okay - always have.

Passions Touch.

Heated by flames of passion,
he gave everything to her desires.
Her kisses lifted him higher than he'd ever been.
While his legs trembled from her touch.
He quivered to the point of explosion,
still, he couldn't give in, not yet;
he wanted to make sure she did likewise...

Seasons of Love.

The biggest mystery
is likened onto seasons game.
We know not whence it comes
but it comes all the same.

In times of passion
colorful winds will blow.
And in times of misgivings,
it helps us to grow.

It's heated like summer;
with its cool soothing nights.
Feisty as a springtime storm
bringing rainbows of delight.

We know not whence it comes
but when it comes, we'll play.
It thrills our delight
in leaving marks
likened to seasonal ways.

Capture and Release.

Words from the heart.
No second guesses.
No worries or strife.
Feelings buried
needing to escape so,
they're ripe for the picking-
so read away.
I've written a thousand poems
with a hundred lines,
each being different
to describe.

The heart races;
furiously beating in memory.
Sputtering to check,
then racing some more.
The mind has found stalemate.
Pausing on things it can't recite.
'Till nightfall comes,
waking me from dream.

And you, you,
step in with comfort.

Waking beside me in throws
only passion can know.
There it is again,
reminiscing of when
a twist of fate awakes
another day...

There, hand in hand
in a world as lovers,
my friend-
there is only one for me.
She feels as I,
loves as I,
and knows the need-
so, she gets it all.

Deeply, slowly, softly;
with all the fiery heat
my lips can press
into her tender heart.

Tasting that which is adorned
is likened unto nectar of gods;
for even they knew the value in its pot.

In its richness, a man finds worth.
Once inside, honey seeps,
waiting to be tasted...

Its flavor holds investigation.
There, a defining moment
between release and capture
tells all.
There we are one.

Fulfillment.

Ask and you shall receive.
Past tense words yet,
meaning the same.
Faith provides insight
to the measurable.
Grace delivers comfort
towards acceptance,
and Joy,
joy brings the smile
in knowing.
Day's aren't over by a long shot,
No!
It has granted purpose in asking
for fulfillment.

Ego.

Ego can be difficult at times.
What's yours is yours,
and what's mine is yours also.
My heart, my soul;
the very breath I breathe is yours.
I can't help not to fathom this feeling so,
make no mistake, I am forever inspired.
Forever will it be in each other.
Life makes it so.

Spellbound.

It's when he stood silently watching-
he knew they had to dance.
He couldn't control her moves,
nor would he even try.
He simply let her be,
and she liked being free.

They met in the middle dancing.
Slowly at first;
till a rhythm was found.
Damn, could they sway.

It stirred the house,
the walls, and floors.
It echoed chambers
opening doors.

Both forget their names,
inside what was found.
They danced with passion-
they became spellbound.

Parents.

Teach your children to remain special
in their own eyes,
and they will show the world who cares.
Who listened to their fears
when a world turned away.

Once Again.

You caused my soul to laugh.
You've made this heart smile.
I'd be honored being a part forever.
And yes, I'd even go an extra mile.
It's because I love you so,
always will.
I'll cherish days we've spent together,
and the many nights alone also.
You are my soulmate, my partner;
once again, I am home.

Morning Joe.

Sitting buck naked on the bed drinking coffee,
and you know what I saw?
It wasn't the radiant body!
It was the sex appeal in her eyes;
each time you took a sip
starring deep into mine.

Educational Merit

'If not for inquiries wit
there could be no imagination
to even out the score.
Therefore early on it was learned
that words alone
meant little to the masses,
where sentences, with phrases
that caught the minds eye were as good,
if not better than those same teachers
had been passing across
as educational merit.'

Learning to See.

Of all the things I'm learning to see.
Like God's children coming into being.
Or like winds tossing, turning,
churning up his seas;
there is nothing more grand
than feeling love's destiny.

Pot of Gold.

A pot of gold
is like dipping your tongue
into a honey trove,
then quivering with every fiber
of your being
anticipating the next taste.

The Hardest Concept.

The mere concept of loving
is the underbelly of what is wrong with society.
Vows are set in order to honor,
and so is this accord set aside to abide in love.

Mutually excepted between right and wrong
is what leaves people tripping over these confines.
So to whom do we owe this great honor?
Is not professing such a thing a bit more
than any person could ever hope to grant?

Honor the vow!
Honor the highest giver of this choice as well.
That is love divulged in its rarest form possible.
And to agree or disagree on the later
is neither greater or lesser to either of the two.

This is where people lose self control.
If one cannot agree,
ask yourself,

Who granted love in the beginning?
And who garnered its very existence
to except this welcoming?

Surely one can find it within themselves
to knowingly expect this concept of divine intervention
as surely as one can see the sun rise to warm the hearts
in which it was given unto.

Writers Block.

The surface closes in
when we learn to breathe.
When we get inside things
we've hidden behind.
Recalling ties binding us
to that which made it so.
Letting them remain intact,
or go away, who knows.
Don't keep crossing bridges if it hurts,
burn 'em down!
However, they may be ones
that'll have to be crossed again
in order to find an ending
to our chapters in life.
These are the pages
in which we do our sums.
Every minute tale documented
with classic twists
that only a writer can pen
to there extreme.

Inspire.

You never know how much someone needs your words.
How much the impact of just a few may change.
So please, all you poets and writers out there—
write your stories, change a life,
brighten a smile; it's never to late to inspire
a new generation of dreamers.

Imagine.

Imagine where we're going.
Imagine where we've been.
A place we've sat for hours,
talking 'bout our sins.

Imagine being set free.
Imagine, and picture our tree.
The bench sat upon,
it awaits you and me.

Imagine a marigold sun setting.
Imagine there's not a cloud in the sky.
Let's reach for the stars, become as they,
for their parts are now ours caught in the eye.

Imagine racing round that tree.
Imagine there's you and me.
Coming together after it's said and done,
laying us to rest on the bench of eternity.

Convoluted Restraint.

How convenient it is to be torn between
freewill and a spirit requiring release?
Rust reminds us corrosion comes;
barbed and sharp as it spreads,
slow and misshaped.

Like lofty thoughts from the soul.
Fruit will always be offered,
and the garden waiting
is to be nurtured.

For love is a growing light;
bright and distanced.
It isn't confined to sight...

Has the body lost its way to eternity?
Or is it confined to an earthen grave?
Once reborn it becomes unrestrained!
Mystifying even, unnamed.
Convoluted, with restraint.

Eons Ago.

You came alive within a touch.
I came alive by it as well.
When was the first time the eyes opened?
And when did the sun shine ever so brightly?
All these things are a mystery.
All these things pass without us.
When was the first time eyes met?
Was there a time more than now to see?
If love not be the answer to desire,
we'd have never asked for it to begin!
Hold me as I hold you.
Touch me the way I feel inside.
Make me wise enough to know this difference.
When was the first time the eyes met?

Believe.

Let me be where you are,
and where you are not.
Let me be a shadow watching
from under a tree long forgot.
Let me be warmth upon your skin.
Never forget I am there.
Never loose the faith I gave.
So feel your way
when you can't see,
and most of all,
always believe.

Autumn Hike.

Hiking one side to the other
can be daunting.
None knows what awaits.
Walk it, cross it,
or be tossed aside–
It'll always be there...
Each has a bridge,
and to each,
a path on the other side.

Held.

If my senses could speak—
they'd shout to a world
wrapped in silence...
For in silence there's solace,
and in solace, peace.
It's nice to be held.

Hopes.

I don't know what lies beyond.
I hope green fields
as far as the eyes can see.
I hope rest awaits,
as well as shallow pools
in which to wade.
I hope comfort finds weary souls.
I can hope for all kinds of things but,
I really don't know...
My faith gives me promise.
My belief fills me with tears of joy
that you, my little grass roller
are there waiting for me.

Sorta' Dementia.

We are every where
and no-where.
We're just out of sight.
Moving as a vesper.
Doing as we'd like.
Bound eternally
to this abode.
We are everything
and nothing.
We are those who loath.
A vision compelling.
A trusting fair.
Reaching for distance
that isn't even there.
Searching corners.
We're in every book.
Closely,
look closely;
we hid behind
that last look.

Chosen.

In a world
that seems make believe;
I'd choose you...
Over and over,
a thousand times over,
and it would still cause a smile.
I know you don't see how!
I know you don't understand why,
and that's okay, just feel;
just be you,
and I'll choose you
over and over again.

Work the Art.

We could walk paths surrounding Caserta,
and my eyes would still only be for you.
My ears listening intently to every word,
clinging onto your delicate tone.
Beauty of the stone statues is stunning but,
not as grand as your eyes meeting mine.
This is where beauty resides,
and here we will remain;
master pieces of
God's creation.

The Fall.

It wasn't the fall that startled me.
It was strength of arms that caught me.
Eyes of a soul I looked into
as my freight faded...

Those were challenging times.
Times for forgiving.
Times for reliving memories.
Can you recall who caught you?
Can you recall the day?
An hour?
Was it sunny or rainy?
Was it worth the fall?

Toppled.

Let words gather dust,
for they must
in order to be understood.

Let them rest in books,
on shelves,
for no one to read.

Let the rhymes be misunderstood,
and let the good in them
never fade away.

Let words gather dust,
for they must.

Let the quill be set aside.
Put the stopper in the bottle,
and let the words rest.

Shed no doubt.

Any second is worth a thousand smiles.
Each lasting years in my soul.
Have I not said,
"You are the gift.
The very purpose in which I breathe.
You are my sun, my moon,
and my star shining forever
over an endless sea.

Highlights.

One second with you
reminds me of past lifetimes.
That forever is forever ours.
The everlasting counterpart
of humble beginnings.
With clouds at our feet,
and wind for song;
singing in tune
to our highlighted
understanding.

Progressions.

The memory remains constant.
Causing me to shake
in a way
a heart shouldn't,
but it does.

My mind and body
gladly gives itself up
to those progressions.

Memories call.
Thoughts prevail,
and my heart is yours;
it gave in.

Kisses Explore.

I read my way across her frame
with each and every kiss.
Every contour was explored.
Nothing was untouched as I read.
Not a scent undiscovered.
Candles flickered softly
off glistening kisses flare.
Vigorously I roamed
from here to there;
reading her bodies heat.
The ecstasy on her face,
as our lips grazed for mere moments,
until her lithe neck began to glow so,
I explored further.
Quivering at what lay below.
Sententious mysteries crying out.
Crying for more than kisses.
I read fully as fingertips explored.
Every recess, every passionate sigh,
every kiss, longed for more.

Take Me Back.

Take me back to cobblestone streets.
Where the only discrepancy is when to meet.
Be it morning, afternoon, or under late night stars.
Be it by a wayside creek, or roadside bazaar.
Take me with you beneath torch lit orchards.
Places outside, to where dreams reward.
Where hands fall into others and speak.
Where hearts collide and begin to peak.
Take me with you, I want to go.
Take me home so I may know -
souls were meant to meet.

Golden.

I look down into times edge
and see us smiling,
playing,
loving the day.
Taking each one as it comes.
Fulfilling each others dreams.
One memory is a treasured embrace
but a thousand,
that's gold.

Laughter.

If laughter be the best medicine,
then set my ribs on fire.
Set my soul to relaxing in harmony.
Who but you could take me higher?
Take me in, fill me.
Laugh with me.

Strong Enough.

If you're strong enough,
look deep into her eyes.
Listen to her as she speaks.
This is where she hides,
this is who she is...
This is where beauty resides.

The Thrill.

I didn't need to love you physically to know you.
That, I learned by looking into your eyes.
That's when I knew I had to have you.
A moments gaze told me everything.
And when you whispered my name,
all I could think of, was yours.

Two P's in a Pod.

She was full of a love that would last forever.
Like rivers of life, continually giving her quotes.
Transcendence flowed outward within a smile.
Like a songbird whispering soft, delicate notes.

He was adventurous, seeking to be known.
Hers was a beauty, worth the wonder of risk.
A preeminence, that needed to be tamed.
Those were the waters reaching out to frisk.

In the light of life's pod a cradling was assured.
Inspiration let love keep this flame from going out.
Reassured two P's exclaimed, "Let's gather it all!
Together we can share, warming those without.

Let's become fresh and vibrant enough to laugh.
Enjoy castles built out of our own broken glass.
Let's rejoice again as one, not as two separate pods.
Today is tomorrows understanding come to pass."

The Eulogy.

The honor was always mine.
The choice was yours.

Dreams made never fade.
Lines broken were chores -
this we gladly did
as reward.

We taught and learned.
We laughed
watching bridges fade.

We never turned away -
for ours was an accolade.

Each supporting the other.
In return, memories.
These are things others can't see -
therefore I wrote this eulogy.

A tribute to all
that's said and done.
A reminder to all
who wish to come.

The honor was always mine.
Now a pinnacle,
set aside
by time.

Clarification.

Just to clarify -
In the writing world,
we can make someone
who it is we wish them to be...
Good, bad, naughty or nice but,
I'll tell you this much;
inside those stories
are pieces that no-one
will ever see.
That's how it should be.
You see me, and I see you.
Hearts calling to another
through a quill.

Spilling Souls

It was never about sex.
It was a finite connection
between two souls that drives one on.
The way they join and roll.
The way they play to music in their soul.
This is what it is about,
and I'd gladly spill it again.

The Lost Child.

I love the way you take hold of me.
Inch by inch,
possessing me at will.
Causing me to surrender
to warm
caressing kisses.
Making me squirm like a child
being told to hold still.
But I never could,
nor will I.
You caused my world to stop
while my head spins with each
and every press then,
you take me in.
Individual kisses flow madly,
and I,
that ever lost child,
want you for my very own.
Don't know what I was searching for
but I found it in your eyes.

Shining Example.

You do more than try.
You set an example to be proud of.
How to look when things turn grim.
How to shine when things go dark.
That's where you shine!
Lighting the recesses of hope.
Showing those to see
prosperity in belief.

I'm always there.

I'm just a thought away.
An emotion arriving in a tear.
A smile, waiting to escape.
So never forget,
I'm always there.

In Bloom.

A single flower blooming
draws much attention
with it's vibrant colors
and fragrances adore.
Where-as a bunch together,
gets oohs and ahh's -
But, become a lone flower flourishing,
and they'll see something special.

Pieces.

Felt like a wilting flower planted along the path of life.
Tiny pieces kept falling until it rained.
Tried to dance but my roots wouldn't motivate.
Then, when I least expected it, sunshine came.
Watched in wonder as those scattered pieces bloomed.
Each blossomed into an enlightening array of color;
now everyone is able to enjoy pieces of me.

Softly.

Love comes in many shapes and forms.
To think otherwise is plain foolishness.
You'll know it is there by a soft smile
or that gentle unknowing tear.

Uplift.

I would cross an ocean for you.
Swim tides of time
just to see you smile.
Walk the blackness of destiny
to hold your hand.
Chase back the years in your eyes
then cry out in relief,
knowing your alive.
May the sun rise to guide us home
no matter how high the tide.

Intensive.

The secret is to listen intently.
Let her secrets fill your soul.
Don't turn away from that trust—
she believes in you.

Deep within.

All I can do is try to be at peace
with my raging thoughts.
Everything will be okay.
I got this!

Embrace.

You know I want you.
How deeply need you,
and when we are separated—
all I have to do is go inside
of memories shared
to feel your embrace.

Listen.

A woman doesn't want to be better—
they wish to be heard.
For no man has suffered more,
nor will anyone give as much.
There are times
when she is far superior but,
she only compliments.
Together anything is possible
as long as both listen.

Awhile, a little, afar.

Aloft-
in a blinded haze.
Afar-
forgetting night has come.
Forward,
ever forward-
pushing the day.
A little-
endless flights.
Fields water the eye.
Alone again.
A little too much.
Water streaming,
clouds beaming-
diving into an aurora.
Afar is the wonder of gifts-
jealousy is somber.
Again, alone,
awaiting night.

The Weight.

If anything can be learned-
let it be caressed by forgiveness.
Be thankful for any given day.
Be gracious for those who surround.
And love, because this is the weight.

Touched.

Promise me
whatever tomorrow brings,
you'll keep our love within.
Let that emotion drive you –
never forget our souls
have touched.

Completed.

I'm secure enough in my love
that time and distance
only make it stronger.
You are my love,
and I, yours.
Our bond is finite —
for together
we are complete.

Declarations.

This heart beats of love.
It pumps memories to mind.
It can't rest. It won't sleep,
and oh, the stories it finds.
It can't forget it,
nor will I resist it-
where-as it guides
this declaration.

Roll Me.

*I don't just want someone to lay me down.
I want someone who'll roll me over many times
while whispering in my ear how wonderful it is
to be touched in such a way.*

Stop.

Stop and feel the sunshine.
Stop and smell the flowers.
Stop and feel the breeze on your skin.
Just stop, and let the world in.

All Yours.

Glad I was able to fulfill a need.
Desire was mine of course but,
the release- all yours.
Unstoppable and yet,
quenchable.

I wonder.

I wonder what it would be like to live a life,
and not be able to dream at all.
To dream, wide awake;
not seeing the meaning behind any of it.

How sad it would be
to never be able to wonder at all.
I wonder what it would feel like
to see everything with such clarity.
And what if no-one could see enough
to dream?

Oh, how happy I am that I can dream.
Sometimes I dream aloud,
becoming outspoken as I look precariously about
into a world full of doubt created by its own fear.

I wonder if I ever told the tale
of things being turned upside down?
And if any could imagine it being turned right over again?

I wonder if heads would spin,
falling out of control?
Would love be poured back into those lost souls?

I wonder about it sometimes,
and then there's you,
yes you, watching every move
with the guidance of a mother hen
keeping close eye on its brood.

I wonder day in and day out before falling asleep
to dream all over again about things
I can only see within the minds eye.
This is where I go
to reconcile what I know to be true,
and that end to things in which
I can never speak aloud.

Patiently.

From the moment I wake,
'till the eyes close,
the moon churns seas,
taking me to where I reside...
Out past the shoals.
Past horizons keep I wait...
Some speak this language-
soft and slow, warm and wild,
heated and rough, yet, untamed...
The earth quakes under my feet;
still, I don't care, I'm here, awake...
Waiting on sunrise to lighten
that which I already know...
'Till the pen be put away.
'Till the coming rays cease-
I await,
patiently.

Illicit Fruit.

Seen it hanging -
dripping wet with its dew.

Desire, passion,
revolving round in waves.

Engulfing.
What is reasoning?
Oh, what to do?

Moving about doesn't help;
it only provokes the fire.
Then for one brief instant -
sanity remains.
Oh, but these flames
keep rising higher.

Reaching out -
there's no point of restraint.
The only thought of will
is to obtain...

A hunger,
a need
to harvest
something so sweet.

The mouth waters in anticipation.

Smelling the essence.
Once tasted –
there's only sweet,
sweet nectar.

Lead us Home.

Time separates,
and for good cause.
It leaves harvested truths behind;
showing us what is real.
Love itself is manifested in it,
while leading us to where we belong.
Do not take this for granted!
Do not sit idly for too long!
It slips a little with each breath.
It grows within, without,
and watches us nurture that river
which flows toward home.

The Gift.

The real gift is when you allow
someone to be themselves....
Then they'll find strength,
along with the will to conquer
anything that comes before them.

In Earnest.

If I caused one smile,
one laugh,
a single tear of joy,
all is not lost...

One doesn't aspire to be great;
only known enough to have stirred
real emotions...

To have inspired others to think,
to smile, even to cry,
then,
all is not lost...

This is writing.
This is who we are.
Artist-
dreaming in earnest.

Forevermore.

Seen a true sunrise with you by my side.
I know now what effervescence feels like.

Upon the door a knocking pounds.
Relentlessly the heart beats aloud.
Once, I failed to head those sounds-
I was a child, had my head in the clouds.
Then it came again- the heart again,
begins to pound.

Telltale signs of rocks strewn at my feet.
Of earth, its weight, pressing down.
This has taught the how and why of it all.
Without missing a beat, smiling,
I gaze into a new sunrise.

Lakes once long gone, are now for bathing.
Valleys seen are lush and green again.
Of all these things I'd wished I had seen-
was this very sunrise washing over me.

So now, here with faith –
I'll answer the door,
and walk into forevermore.

Unity.

Sometimes -
we need not even speak.
We utter the same things.
Each picturing different ways yet,
we are the same.

Inside, are those same emotions -
our footprints are laid deep in this sand.
Long before we'd even crossed it.
This is the unity that binds;
this is love.

Confessions.

I must confess the truth;
you were the only one to ever get in!

Most knew of me,
or at least,
parts of me.

But you, you
I gave full introduction;
I let you know the inner workings.

You now knew what made me tick.
Why I felt,
and acted as I did.

Granted —
I was a scared kid,
but, at least
I tried.

The Heart Confides.

Time waits.
Patience participates.
All one and the same
while the heart confides.

Never to be forgotten.
Always and forever.
Acting on impulse;
finding a light inside.

Shine if you feel it.
Believe it cause it's true.
As above, so is it below.

It is both life and death;
dark and light.
Pulling, ever pulling -
on hearts that confide.

Into Memory.

It was a day like any other.
Sunshine mixed with clouds
as I awoke thinking of you.
There in my subconscious
was your face,
smiling as it always does.

Mine
was a morning of silence,
for in the making
were visions of our love.

At the heart of all these things,
again, was your smile.
Ever brighter,
out shining the very clouds
that tried to obscured my vision.

Without this;
I would be asleep -
which isn't bad mind you,

it was that,
I just wanted you there.

Snoring your little snores.
Tossing and turning
from your too heated frame but,
I can only imagine because,
you are there,
and I am here,
looking at a smile
pressed into memory.

My Sunshine.

To the ray of sunshine warming me,
I give thanks for being here.
How could I face the day
without such warmth.

Tenor.

It would never be seen;
that, in which should be.

In fact, it was that
in which couldn't,
that held things together
all along.

It was in that
which was felt,
what was known,
what's held together;
is what helped
keep things calm.

Sparks casting glints
over shadows of doubt.
Smiles of reassurances,
none should go without.

This is what made music.
So sing, sing your song.

Carry it with you as you go.

Sensing only now,
the music was our words.

Tears.

A man sees a light in the eyes.
Feels a warmth growing inside.
Lets it then burst forth,
with tears of joy.
And when they begin to flow;
he recalls where he wishes to be...
There, he is loved truly
for who he is.

Restraint.

I've shown love with compassion.
Passion when necessary.
But, if I hold on to tight;
I could loose it all.
Was it too little too late?
Of that, I'm unsure.
Therefore, the right amount
of restraint is needed
to keep the heart safe.

Last Love.

Have I told you that when I see you,
I feel all warm and fuzzy inside.
Kinda like a tingling sensation
running through my veins
for the very first time.

You understand the feeling...

That first kiss,
from your first love.
Never will it be the last kiss but,
you will be my last love.

To My Reader.

I write one line at a time;
much of life is the same.
I sing and I dance.
Hell,
I even cry still,
I place no blame.

How long has it been
since a page was written?
How long?
I wonder if they could ever be unwritten?
Or will they ever be read?

Each to there own
are nothing but lines scribbled.
And yet,
they're nothing without a binding
to pull things tight.

I often wonder,
looking up at the stars
as they rehearse.

Far and away
in that big blackish thing
we call the universe.
I know there's more
than meets the eye so,
I write.

I chase words in harmony,
pulling hearts towards the light.
If for nothing else
than to see these stories
come to life.

Yes,
these are pleasing things so,
I fill pages to surprise
my reader.

Forever your Poet.

The real splendor is waking.
Knowing there is still love
left in the world.
That the gift
which was given
hasn't completely died.
This is what has been shown.
Therefore,
I am forever your poet.

A Rub.

When the heart is opened to love
it can never close fully again.
It will sing out loud,
lighting a way
for others to see and gather;
hoping a little may rub off.

Bitter Sweet.

Seen honey dripping from a spoon.
Drop by drop it fills the cup.
Always liked sweeter things.
Slowly bending in,
I lick it up.

They say coffee is bitter.
Claim it stings the tongue.
Yet, honey in all its flavor—
soothes as it runs.

Take the cup!
Drink it up.
Days are growing few.
What to do?

Fidgeting fingers
find the gold.
It's soothing,
satisfying—

nothing is greater
than not feeling old.

Oh, you know what to do!

Pull away slowly.
Release this calming storm.
Touch it,
taste it,
now
smile once more.

Sweets belong to the eyes,
and when lips meet,
there is never a retreat-
love cries for more.

My Own River.

Want a shot of whiskey so bad I can taste it.
Taken away by a heartache that won't quit.
Lord, I've taken everything thrust upon me.
I've been angry, cried,
even got lost enough to see.

Regret was never inside for too long.
Now, I look back on an eager life gone.
How many tears must fall before I see?
How many lifetimes must pass without song?

I've been left alone to remorse.
It was my little worry of sorts.
Times change, things pass,
or so the saying goes.
Many a dream has washed away
in these throes.

Imaginations running rampant for the door.
Tears keep falling for a love that needed more.
This happened as I followed closely in the rear.

And yet,
going forward isn't always clear!

Now listen!
Some times it's good to cry!
So, let them fall
from that wall of pride.

Continue walking
over this kind of inequity.
Crystal clear it becomes
searching for tranquility.

Swim out of this river of fear.
Echoes only cast sounds,
the anchor is clear.

Let the future cleanse the cheeks.
Wade round, someday
these rivers will meet.

Tossing, turning,
no-one ever believes.

Where these currents will carry but,
we'll see.

Back inside, dreams often slide,
underneath it all, hazel eyes cry.

My Forever in a Day.

Be my forever in a day.
Be it simply by holding hands.
Standing quietly,
or watching me sway.

Be my forever,
my forever in a day.

Welcome me as if I
could fulfill no more.

Cherish these words
as if there could be no more.
I could have asked for anything,
I asked for a day.
After all I'm a baby-
learning to answer a door.

I still seek refuge in memory.
I still seek a hand to hold me still,
time is an obtrusive demon creeping away.

*Yet, it cannot touch
what I have –
my forever,
forever in a day.*

For You I write.

When I think of you,
I write my hearts desire.
I wish for everything to come true.
I know that it won't but,
I wish it for you anyway;
this is why I put pen to the page.
This is called coming of age.

Memories Touch.

Grand memories
never fade too far.
They resides deep inside,
moving the heart.
Sharper ones touching
like a dull blade;
cutting their way through everything but,
they remain steady -
constantly embedding.
Coming out at will,
to touch.
And sometimes,
sometimes,
they heal everything.

Note to Self.

Dear self,

Slap yourself silly
when you screw up.
Love hardily
when you wake,
and remember,
always remember
if you don't have
anything nice to say -
Shut Up.

Poetic Converse.

Tears come to the eye
when emotions arise.
Moving the mind deep,
even in sleep,
they soothe,
they create,
they motivate,
and then they touch —
yes, they touch the heart,
these are tears of joy,
of sorrow,
of fear but.
there here,
reminding us
that we are human
after all.

My Everything.

She was everything I needed.
The voice, the smell of her hair.
I couldn't turn away.
I tried but, she wouldn't let go.
And be that as it may;
I never wanted her to anyway.

Passion Play.

I found the bean
and rolled it all day.
Romped and romped,
ruffled the hay.

The frenzy was electrifying.
Hidden fires flared up,
then I squeezed the handles
of my buttercup.

Stretched and squirmed.
Got tied in a knot.
Got pushed to the ground,
What else have you got?

A scratch, a nibble,
a run through the hair.
In the heat of the moment
we didn't care.

The grass was warm
under the sun.
We laughed, giggled.
Oh, what fun.

Hours passed by.
We just couldn't stop.
So I pulled back on the reins
and went straight to the top.

Covered in sweat.
Self control was a toy.
Don't know how long we lay
smiling in joy.

We knew not the time.
Nor did we care.
Passion lives forever.
Man!
I messed up your hair.

Sweet Love.

Sweet is being a light
that sparks another's eye.
In being who you truly are.
Place that love back inside the heart;
you may find this is who you are.
Where true beauty hides.

Swirls.

You poured me into a cup
then stirred it round.
Didn't notice you climbing in
'till the heart was found.
Then, as its swirling subsided
we came face to face.
Smiling like children
that had found their place.
There in the bottom
of that cup we lay,
so tease me baby,
swirl away.

Sweet Inspiration.

My sweet little inspiration
grow with me, teach me.
Love me for me,
and never let go.

Soul to Heal.

Times passing in an influx.
There are no words to describe it,
as waves push back against
eternity's shores...
Some things are unexpected.
Love is felt for a soul to heal.
Watching movements.
Swaying endlessly.
Waters warming.
Slowly healing.
Love this feeling.
It's deeply embedded.
Eternity
is what the soul feels
when it is loved
from soul to heel.

River dance.

Reeds lined up and down.
Buried deep and abound.
Tumbling stones,
constant sways.
Oh, the rivers dancing
thoughts invade.

Cool, clear-
inviting even.
Slow and fast,
it's hardly an even pace.

Washed by a shore.
Polished the runes.
They're unique in a way.

Sit back,
and enjoy the view.
Take your time.
What's seen surprises.
Walk these uneven shores.

Follow them into the sea.
Endless is the horizon.
Endless,
are a dreamers dreams.

Passion Wins.

Passion comes from within.
Love from without.
Eyes sparkle openly
when it comes out.
Passion touches.
Entwines one to another.
Love makes it whole.
When the heart listens,
passion wins.

One last kiss.

Exasperated at the departure.
Watched you walk away.
The heart sink's, and leaps all at once.
In the instance you turn,
bringing me one last kiss.

One man band.

Music's playing in his head.
Is it an orchestra,
some jazz?
Nope,
circus music instead.
Bee bopping along;
the musics grand.
Everything's forgotten,
lost-
no footing,
no band.
No violin,
no drum,
not even a guitar.
Oh no,
here it comes,
the kazoo,
or was it a passing car?
He's moving.
He's prancing.
Love him or not-

it's a rhythm
he ain't got.
He's lost,
he's digging the tune.
Eye's are wandering.
What's next?
The moon?
The chorus -
ever perfect.
The rhythm -
oh, so fine.
Damn it all,
he's lost his friggin' mind.
He's dancing to a thumpin'.
Bouncin' to the humpin'.
Heard the music too clearly,
it's a steady
rumpa pum pumpin'.
Can't blame him.
Can't shame him.
And how'd you fare?
Did you hear the kazoo?

Green eyed monster.

Was all done with the green one.
Always seemed to be chasing him away.
Life's desires move in a timely way.
Maybe it's all for fun?

A little thought coursing these veins.
Boiling the chambers of pride.
Tried to resist but cried inside.
Couldn't push away that demons rain.

It rolls an ugly head.
It causes me to sway.
It walked in again, ruining a delightful day.
Now, it's a fiery red,

Take what it gives, or pass the stone.
It's made its point and longs and longs.
Waking to see where a heart belongs.
I forgot what it was to be truly, alone.

Forgiveness.

The very same moment you asked;
it was given, and done for you.
Remember, when looking at another;
they also grow from what you do!

Devotion.

I hope to inspire through faith.
Enlighten with my love.
One day it'll be recognized
for what I truly was;
a devoted writer
with a love larger
than himself.

Beholden.

Feel, reach, care...

Touch the impossible dream.

Used to look in the mirror
only to see a reflection;
now I see truth...

What's good in life is love.
What's good without it?

Now beholden-
you may begin to live.

A Ride to Remember.

I could never promise
a perfect world.
Nor a perfect life,
because,
I wasn't.

One thing I do know is,
I can promise a ride to remember.
Something to look back upon.
Something to make you smile.

So climb into the seat-
take my hand;
hold it until the sunsets
on us both
and wake us
when tomorrow comes.

Blossoms in May.

Oh, she was worth the time!
And all the effort that came with it.
She always managed a smile,
even when I was a shit.
She seen more than I;
for I was no great prize.
But I was funny, charismatic,
and well, just down right pleasing
on the eye.
I was a huge pain in the butt.
I liked things a certain way.
Still, our love flourished—
blossoming, like flowers in May.

Shine On.

You may never notice
but others will;
that the glow is different
when someone loves you.

You'll shine like stars -
feeling this kind of warmth.
Then you'll cast it outward,
for others to enjoy.

Begin Anew.

Life begins anew
when you find what you're after.
Nothing else matters,
not time, the world;
even fears will disappear.
That's the best feeling
anyone can give.
When they've given hope, faith,
and the grace to carry yourself.
That's when life begins.

Forgotten, forever, free.

You believed in this life,
in me; on this very plain.
You've felt the next- pulling.
You've seen the rift in between,
placing a veil over the scene.
All recollection has been removed.
Free will is placed in its stead.
All complimentary complacency
has been chosen.
Let life fill this feeling forever.
You are free once more to beam.

Magic.

Firmly believed in a destination.
A place where we all belong.
Surrounded by those filled with love.
I've heard it in a child's voice.
Oh, how they believe.
How they longed to run free.
And don't we all!
I knew of such a place!
I've seen it in a dream.
Then I woke-
realizing it was here.
Heaven on Earth.
Live it well.

The Story-line.

I was glad to see the story was read.
I was also happy it helped.
Appreciated the confidence bestowed.
May it be returned with love.
Remember how the story was writ.
All the people that wrote lines to it.
The good, bad, well, even the ugly too;
it's what kept the story real.

A Poets Fire.

Forever a poet wistfully dreams.
Of mountains, orchards,
and cool running streams.
Writing of nights,
under moonlit skies,
all while thinking on tomorrows
relentless tides.
Today he writes of you,
and everything you are -
for his greatest stories come alive
beneath those stars.
The way they twinkle -
enlightening to inspire,
and if words are not enough -
touch his heart,
set it on fire.

Between Then and Now.

Seems I found time you couldn't.
Placed it between then and now.
Loved every second, every minute;
spent every ounce to know this.

Memories-keep flooding the mind.
Oh yes, I've found time again.
Call it crazy if you will.,
I'm a country boy
through and through.

Love long walks;
it gives time to reflect.
And yet,
memories keep filling the mind.

Found time once more-
I think of you;
I recall emotions
long pushed aside.

Placed them between
then and now.

Sometimes I cry out loud.
Yes,
I even do that too.

Memories come and go.
They make me wonder
that day after day I,
I was just a fool.

Subconscious Sacrifice.

I understand how David must have felt,
for he loved unconditionally.
He dealt with emotions some only consider.

But I'm not David—
I'm simple and humble,
with a faith that binds me to such things.
I have a heart that yearns.
A soul that screams while I dream,
wearily.

I've been hurt,
marginalized.
Rationalized
with words over doubts
others can't comprehend.
This is the subconscious merit
of sacrifice.

Feeding Fire.

Escaping the hearth.

Devouring,
taken aback from its heat.

Embers from coals simmering;
I am aroused
by this inferno I keep.

A sea of flames arise
from all sides.

Passions hot spot
begins to burn.

Releasing slowly -
madness is blinding yet,
it yearns.

Fire is often tricky.

Its real power is in the smoke.

All sultry while desire looms;
clouded and darkening,
its time to remove the yoke.

The charming softness of it all.

Rolling away in hot spells.
Suddenly,
a heavy sigh,
fills this deepening well.

Fully intact.

Heating the moment.

It's smothering.

it's a killer warmth that starts.

Turning,
reeling inside.

Damn!
That's a pretty scar
on a heart.

Empty Spaces.

Smooth walls -
glaring.
Soothing chimes
for sharing.

Empty mantles
with foreign spaces -
full of hand me down things.

Footprints echo in silence.
No one ever comes - it's empty.

Tracing floors,
walls are uninviting.
Pushing back
against forevermore.

Swinging wildly while often smiling.
Running through revolving doors.

Emptied and hallowed;
forgotten and swallowed.
Darkness creeps in spaces left behind.
Often wonder
why God made thunder-
'till those faces come a calling;
faces,
hidden within the mind.

Simple Satisfactions.

Relief,
pride,
pleasure.
A few simple words
for satisfaction.

When somethings done right-
you know it.
It brings gratification.

Little comforts,
well being.
Some things worth while to see.

Peace of mind,
heavy sighs,
are often more
than meets the eye.

Believe in me
and I'll believe in you.

All our indemnity's are sown.

Have you ever thought about it?

Someone payed,
somewhere,
sometime.

This doesn't mean one should quit.
So reach out
and touch those goals.

Two Sunsets.

If there were two sunsets in my rear view;
one would always be watching over you,
always chasing, the other,
keeping you warm.
Both would never fade.
Never abandon you
in time of need.
May you always be able to look up,
feel its embrace, along with the essence
that takes solace in creation

Wind in the sky.

A long,
long time ago;
there was a pilot
sailing the sky.

Alone,
just enjoying the ride...
Sailing shores of know-where.
There are no coincidences;
only choices.

And those choices
lead to a beacon,
which always shine bright.

Because,
whether it ends or begins;
its light flutters
across the surface
of the sky.

*Soothing,
as he races on.*

*It cannot be forgotten,
for there it is again,
another gust,
moving,
another cloud now
passes by.*

The Consequence.

A smile that engulfs
and entwines
with its overpowering price
takes
its very breath
from sounds
of resignation.

It's filled with tears
from cold night's
in silence.

Slipping further away for mercies sake.
But it comes again, to ensue.
Teaching new ways to be,
new ways to see
while peering past
this gentleness of gloom.

Oh,
I know the consequence.

I know.
I feel smiles from across the way.
Always close,
never far —
together rising and falling
like shooting stars
being wished upon.

Leaving Things Behind.

May you always be in good standing.
May your heart always remain pure.
May you find true happiness
as these words find you.
May you always be honest,
because there will never be
another like you.
Reflections are all we can leave so,
may they all shine.

Drifting.

The culture of the day doesn't love, love.
The idea however, with its fleeting charm,
it's eager giddiness, now that, it craves.
Sometimes it catches itself wandering in;
slowly drifting in thought
of how wonderful the concept is and yet,
it cannot latch hold of that in which
it doesn't understand.
If it isn't welcomed in life,
how can it be accepted in the end?
And to expect otherwise
is the very basis
for misunderstanding
what it truly gives -
hope.

Silent Paradox.

The road was long,
winding,
and lonely.
Through the clatter of footsteps
I learned to listen
to this silence.
I didn't come to exist,
I came to live.
To explore,
and to wonder.
To give into this experience-
as if silence was an embrace
hidden within
itself.

From the inside.

I came,
I saw,
I felt it all.
I lived
and I cried,
then I went inside.
I wanted to read every page,
the prologue with it's chapters.
I wished to be in the story line,
hidden within every line.
Recorded inside the books spline.
Then,
forever,
I would be alive.
I would be there for others to explore.
For others to know...
That's why I went inside;
here,
I am known.

Waving Bye.

Thinking of you.
Your love lingers
in my heart,
every hour
of every day.
I can still remember
the way you were.
I can still recall
your laughter,
and things you would say.
In memory
I've been thinking,
one day
I'll be at your side.
Some day
Jesus will come for me,
till then,
I'll be waving bye.

The Resolve.

So long forgotten.
So long dreams
hide within reality.
Reasonable doubt
prickles the nape -
there's no escape.
No stairs to climb.
No reassurances this time,
There's only me,
and I question
the resolve.

Knowing.

Was never one that cared too much
if anyone liked my works or not but,
there was one I always tried to impress.
Always knew the face, and they weren't
much for commenting either,
I knew they were watching.
Silently from the sidelines.
Felt it in my heart.
That's what kept me going;
it was knowing they were there.

About the Author:

G.W. Crider resides with his family in lower rural Michigan, and is a heavy equipment operator by trade where most of his days are spent enjoying the great outdoors. Besides spending time with his family, he enjoys woodworking and especially writing. He has been writing since early childhood, and continues to write short stories and poetry.

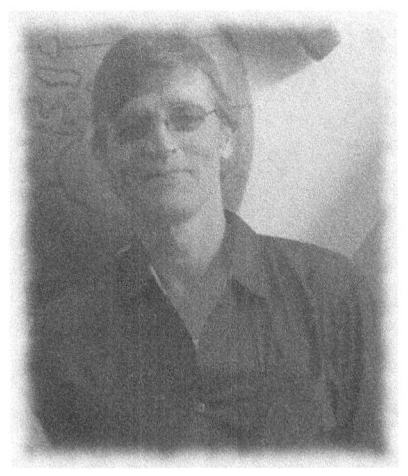

Other works by G.W.Crider
that can be found on Amazon include;

Denouement Before the Reign.
Poetry in Motion.
Spiritually Speaking.
The Sonnet Project.
Unworthy Scribbles.
Poetry in Narrative.
When Shadow's Disappear.
Compositions of a Fragmented Mind.
Dead River Falls.

www.ingramcontent.com/pod-product-compliance
Lightning Source LLC
Chambersburg PA
CBHW070638220526
45466CB00001B/217